Best Ways to Invest Money during COVID-19

M. L. PILGRIM

If you are looking for investment that offers you inflationary protection and that reduces your investment risk significantly, precious metals such as gold, silver, and platinum (amongst others) is the way to go. Unlike paper money, precious metals have a finite supply and you cannot print more of them, and because of this, precious metals offer authentic insurance against political and financial upheavals. This book will share about the ff:

WHAT ARE PRECIOUS METALS?
WHY YOU SHOULD INVEST? - THE UPSIDE AND DOWNSIDE
WHO SHOULD INVEST?
WHAT PRECIOUS METALS SHOULD YOU INVEST IN?
WAYS TO INVEST IN PRECIOUS METALS
CONCLUSION- WHEN SHOULD YOU INVEST?

The primary aim of this eBook is to open young investors' eyes to the infinite possibilities of investment in precious metals. This eBook shows you that you have the time advantage of youth and the ability to take on more risks, and that these advantages can help you make better and bigger investment profits, whether you choose to invest in gold, palladium, copper, silver, or platinum and whether you choose to invest in coins, bars, rounds, or precious metal ETFs.

So take action, and scan the QR CODE and Subscribe to our newsletter for more updates!

Best Ways to Invest Money during COVID-19

TO MY WIFE AND MY SON, THIS BOOK IS FOR YOU.

Copyright © 2020 by M.L. PILGRIM

ISBN 979-8-6541-8618-8 (Paperback)

Cover Design by M.L. PILGRIM

All rights reserved. No part of this book may be reproduced without written permission of the copyright owner, except for the use of limited quotations for the purpose of book reviews.

This book is not intended as a substitute for the directions and advice of professionals. It is merely written with the intention to help in the process of the readers.

Contents

Introduction 8
Chapter 1 9
COVID-19 effects on global economy 9
Chapter 2 12
COVID-19 and personal investment, an overview 12
Chapter 3 16
Real estate investment during COVID-19 16
Chapter 4 18
Gold investment during COVID-19 18
Chapter 5 20
Investment in FOREX during COVID-19 20
Chapter 6 23
Which is better during COVID-19: Investing in Forex, Gold, or Real Estate? 23
Chapter 7 25
Various ideas for "Online" Work – Invest in Yourself 25
Chapter 8 28
Experts' advices and overview 28
Conclusion 31
Bibliography 32
About the Author 34
Books by this Author 35

Introduction

First of all, I want to thank you for purchasing this book, and I can assure you that you will not regret it.

We provide a short yet very informative summary on what you can do during this pandemic, stemming out of the bad feelings you may get and the fear of losing your savings among all this panic, we included in the next few lines great and proven steps to not only protect your money but also to grow it!

At anytime, whether there is a crisis or not, there will always be some opportunities out there, the smart investor is the one who seize these opportunities and even create them, if you want to be one of the intelligent investors and take the first step towards money making, you are in the right place. We are here to lead your path, as in times of crises people will definitely need the advices of experts.

Your will to invest money is enough for us to give our best to hand you the perfect guidelines on how to do it, now let's start the work!

Chapter 1

COVID-19 effects on global economy

The spread of the new Coronavirus or COVID-19 appears to have affected all aspects of life in all the countries attacked, especially the economic sector, where a state of stagnation in production and export prevailed.

So, what is the impact of the Coronavirus on the global economy, and what is the extent of the losses if it continues to spread?

Coronavirus will disrupt the production processes in many countries of the world, due to the imposition of the blockades, which occurred because of the insanely high rate of spread, and that the new world order will change, and new poles will appear.

The global giant companies that manufacture medicines will take a major role in the international community, as will the restructuring of international institutions working in the humanitarian field, and this will work to reshape international bodies and blocs in the world.

There will be a kind of slowdown in the production processes, but not by the large size, pointing out that China, after overcoming the crisis, has returned to production, and therefore it will benefit from the experience, because its production will be directed to countries that have been infected with the virus.

In this context, There are many countries whose budgets will be badly affected, as a result of its fight against the virus, in addition to that, there will be a breakdown of industries, and this results from the slowdown in national production, during the current coming period.

These losses will continue as long as the virus continues to spread, and even after it, it is not easy for countries to reprogram themselves, especially since there are countries suffering from crises in the first place, expecting that at the end of this year, the spread of the virus will be curbed in all countries of the world.

Coronavirus has negative effects on the global economy, for example, in China, from which it spread, there was a decline of 14% of GDP (Gross Domestic Product) during the first and second months.

One of the losses incurred by China is that it has suspended most factories and workers, and the state has paid the salaries and wages of workers, in addition to the fact that the Chinese central bank has allocated 370 billion dollars to fight COVID. And since China is major supply chain source of the world, the rest of the economies who depended on it are impacted as well.

One of the countries that were affected is Brazil, as one of the countries that have wide trade markets with China, in addition to the major international companies such as (Apple) and (Ford) for cars. Also, traders suffered billions of losses on the global stock exchange, and the decline in oil prices, as the barrel of oil reached below $ 0 !! That happened on April 20, 2020.

In addition to that, the transport between countries, as well as sports, has been affected, as the leagues in most European countries have stopped, as Italy, England and Spain, and this leads to severe losses related to clubs, player salaries and advertisements.

All this pushed the World Bank to confirm that the world could go through a great recession, such as what happened in the nineteen thirties, and that if the pandemic continues, the recession means high prices and a shortage of goods in most countries, and it is expected that the losses will be in billions of dollars.

Chapter 2

COVID-19 and Personal investment, An Overview

Economic crises usually hits the whole world's economy, this happens as waves of recessions or what economists call "shocks" to the global market. But still, there are some investors who can seize once in a life opportunities during such conditions, even if it seems impossible to gain profits at such times, some people can force the market to act into their favours and that is by only one thing, adapting. This is a way to create opportunities out of nothing even at the darkest times.

If you read the history of any of the wealthy all around the world you will easily notice that there is some basic guides from which many have gained dozens of dollars, one of these rules say that times of crises may unexpectedly provide the best opportunities for making money.

But what really happens is that some people get really afraid when relying on this theory. This can also be explained especially during the current crisis of COVID-19 as the unprecedented nature of this particular crisis that all countries are going through will probably take months to find a solution to this virus.

But regardless of the nature of any crisis, there are always the ones who refuse to give up to those fears and follow that rule believing it is the only way to succeed, it is only about how to see the opportunities that these crises offer and if you cannot see them you can simply create them.

In situations like the one we are having now, the assets' prices sharply decrease or remain preserved and few other assets rise in price, the art of investment rises at its best during such circumstances, as the real super investors can identify which assets will rise so they buy them before their prices explode. And other investors prefer to look for these assets which is about to witness a huge price drop, they predict this and sell these assets before the fall happens.

Other investors seek a very different third option which is to keep the liquidity of money within their hands, they tend to wait and avoid any risks, so they stay away from the investment market as a whole until the very right time.

The authors of this theory reinforce their view that history always indicates that every crisis has a climax, and therefore it will soon decline in severity or disappear completely, except rarely. Investing in entrepreneurial ideas and innovative projects may be one of the best ways to invest in times of crisis, and this may come as a substitute for traditional investment and resorting to safe havens such as gold, dollars, and real estate, although the real estate sector is always described as the safest market, especially as it is the investment that may get sick but it never dies due to this or that crisis.

As for the answer to the point that crises create wealth, is it real or an illusion? The ideal answer here is that crises create wealth for those who are good at seizing opportunities. For example, in 2011, Warren Buffett invested $ 5 billion in Bank of America after losing half of its market value as a result of the financial crisis.

What is more important here is the behaviour that must be demonstrated by individuals who want to invest, they should be calm and manage their net savings wisely and patiently, these are among the most important tools that must be activated in such times.

Also, we should not keep up with the trendy fashion in the sense that you should not proceed with your investments according to the instinct of the herd, especially in the fields of stocks and real estate. Also, do not put all eggs in one basket, no matter how tempting one of the investments is, diversifying the investment portfolio and investment sectors is usually described as one of the basics of every successful investor, because it is simply enough to protect your money from being lost completely.

Avoid loans as much as possible.

With regard to forms of safe investment in times of crisis and how to use that to maximize your savings, one of the most desirable solutions in times of economic crises is gold, as gold, and all kinds of precious metals that can be purchased such as silver, diamonds and jewellery in general, is an economic anti-crisis tool. And economic fluctuations, and its global value represents a physical safety barrier for those who possess it in times of crisis. In many cases, it is considered the best investment after the crisis.

The second form of investment in times of crisis is ownership of assets, which is one of the areas of investment that must be exercised with caution. As assets are distinguished by retaining their original value over time, they are therefore considered a safe investment that is not affected by the deteriorating economic situation in the country. One of the best choices in this case is definitely buying space for construction permits, then agricultural land, and finally real estate.

As for the third form of investment, it is the trade of raw materials. It is one of the commercial solutions that can provide your family with the basic monthly income. Here we use the original rule (not to maintain cash) as a main strategy in the buying and selling practitioner, so do not sell for the future and try to reduce storage times.

As for investing in the stock market in times of crisis, resorting to shares of local private companies is tantamount to suicide and amortization of your savings, but choosing shares for government joint stock banks or companies that supply raw materials can be a better investment. The purchase of government bonds is also the safest choice on the stock exchange, but it is also the least profitable, as governments are the most trusted entity in the financial market, by which the investor guarantees to recover the value of their bond even with the deterioration of the economy; certainly this is a general principle, if we are talking about an active stock exchange in origin and a country that has a balance of confidence.

In the end, it is safe to say that individuals' decision to invest during a crisis or an economic recession is very difficult, and taking that decision differs considering the type of the market and the country's economy. We will discuss each of investment methods mentioned above in details in the next chapters.

Chapter 3

Real estate investment during COVID-19

Real estate is one of the safest and most common investment markets, as it includes different uses and secured future, there is residential real estate, commercial real estate, farms, factories, and many others, which makes the size of the impact of COVID-19 on them unequal, also, the real estate investment's goals are diversified, there is investment in income generating real estate, and there is real estate development and there are real estate for long-term-appreciation, and therefore the effect of the virus on them cannot be equal.

Also, the fear that tenants will not meet the rent will not be quick due to the varying timing of entitlement to the rent, which is mostly annual. To know the true impact of the crisis on the real estate sector, you must know the actual damage and the duration of that crisis, which is caused by the quarantine, the closure of 70% of shops and companies, and the reduction of working hours, which undoubtedly has a negative impact on some economic sectors.

The precautionary measures taken by countries to reduce the spread of the Coronavirus will lead to the extension of construction schedules for longer periods as a result of reducing the number of workers on the site of work, in addition to reducing the number of working hours because most of the work is done during the day, during the quarantine.

But do not forget that there are sectors that either benefited from that crisis, or that the impact of the crisis on them is minimal, and everyone will return to their work and everything will return to its previous shape in the future.

In experts' opinion, this crisis will continue for a temporary period followed by prosperity. All the crises that occurred globally, were followed by a global trend towards safe shelters for investment, which is real estate and gold, because the risk ratios are small, and the real estate will remain the safe store of value, and this is what will happen after the end of Corona nightmare.

Chapter 4

Gold investment during COVID-19

The fundamentals of investment require that the amount invested is nothing more than a financial surplus after securing basic needs, paying debts, etc.

Even the investment in general has some fixed conditions, it is not correct to put everything you own in only one investment, but you must diversify and distribute the funds to more than one sector and field. When investing in gold, it is better that the share of gold in total investments should be between 5% and 10%, for the purpose of diversification, as gold does not produce any periodic returns.

It is true that no one has a magic ball to know the future, but technical analysis can be used to predict the study of the price behaviour of gold. We expect gold prices to rise to the previous record level of $ 1920 an ounce in the long run, but after going through a stage of corrections.

In detail, the actual journey of the rise of gold began before the outbreak of the Coronavirus, specifically with the breach of the level of $ 1370 an ounce in June 2019 because it was a strong resistance area that gold tried to breach over the past six years.

When gold rose after exceeding the areas of resistance mentioned above, it was able to rise to the areas of $ 1560 an ounce, and then began a short profit gaining wave of about 7%.

What happened after that was worthy of attention, as gold trades are witnessing quick profit-gaining after penetrating each resistance. After going up to $ 1700 levels, it witnessed a decline of about 15% to $ 1450 an ounce.

Then the rise from the regions of $ 1450 exceeding the resistance areas of $ 1700, recording a new level at $ 1750 an ounce.

It is clear that gold is witnessing profit gaining operations with every resistance being penetrated, so it is expected that profit gaining operations of an ounce of gold will occur in the future to levels between $ 1580 and $ 1550 (where the CCI - Commodity Channel Index, which is a very common tool for traders in identifying cyclical trends- indicator shows strong signs of overbought) and then rise again towards $ 1800 then followed by the historical summit of gold at $ 1920 during the second quarter of 2020. As for long-term technical expectations, it depends on the extent of gold penetration of its historical peak of $ 1920, which will aim to rise successfully to a range of about $ 2160 and then $ 2440 an ounce!

This positive scenario for gold moves fails with the monthly closing below the levels of $ 1500 an ounce.

The bottom line is that gold may rise towards $ 1900 an ounce after it is exposed to some corrections, while an increase in the price of an ounce above the levels of $ 1900 may open the door for gold above levels of $ 2000 an ounce. And these expectations remain valid as long as prices do not close below $ 1500 levels per ounce (monthly closing).

In the end, dear reader, you are the master of your decision.

Chapter 5

Investment in FOREX during COVID-19

Large banks and big financial institutions have recently dominated most of the foreign currency trading, but a slight change took place concerning the nature of investment during the last few months, according to some surveys, about 6 million investment accounts were recorded, and it was just 1.5 million in 1997. As a result, the new-to-market companies started with a competition with the major financial institutions in serving investors. This is sponsored by the rapidly developing technology and who won from this context? Fortunately, the customer.

This competition is held between two different types of companies, the ones that deal with the public and those which do not, also there is another side which is online companies, this last one has reduced some investment costs to the limit that can enable the individual investor to have his independent investment strategy in the market of Forex trading.

When some market experts were asked about this, they said that all Forex investors should know that this market is a simple way to access the exchange currencies market, this is defined by the process of buying a currency for instance in exchange for selling another currency, while all global currencies' value change following some indications, all currencies there are traded as pairs, euro-dollar, yen-dollar, and even the rupees.

Few years ago, this business was only available to large banks and financial institutions, but the recent technological explosion allowed small traders to participate in Forex trading through online platforms. The Forex market is open 24 hours a day, and for five days a week.

But now, online trading has reached a whole new stage as this market now is available to anyone from small and to experienced investors. You may be surprised to know that Forex trading has become one of the largest financial markets around the world as trading volume of this market reached $ 1.5 trillion!

Given the current numbers, investors can enjoy some huge profits in the Forex market that may exceed the stock's, and this can open a new door for many to earn their livings from home.

Let's return to the basic topic. Today, most experienced traders are more willing to trade Forex more than stocks, if we talk with numbers, there are around 4,500 shares listed in New York stock exchange, and another approximately 3,500 shares listed in the NASDAQ Stock Exchange. On the other side, the Forex market has four main markets and about 34 currencies to trade in .

Forex investors have the complete freedom to focus only on major currencies or to choose other ones. Forex trading is actually special with its simplicity and freedom, it erases some obstacles that you can find in the stock for example.

Forex trading has some obvious advantages as its availability, simplicity and being a very respectful option that does not require huge capital. In addition to all that, Forex market is also special in terms of cost. It is very economical in terms of trading fees. In general, if you want to trade shares you will have to pay fees ranged between $ 7.95 - $ 29.95 per trade when you use online brokers, it may even exceed $ 100 when seeking traditional brokers. On the opposite side, these commissions are directly related to the quality of services you get from the broker, these services usually reach its peak with traditional brokers. The trading services include an access to analysis techniques and recommendations of experts and others. In Forex, brokers usually charge very small commissions on your trades that are almost negligible.

Chapter 6

Which is better during COVID-19: Investing in Forex, Gold, or Real Estate?

Many investors ask: which investment field is the most appropriate to the current situation in COVID-19 pandemic? Is it gold, currencies, dollars, or real estate?

If you want to find an answer, you must first know some basics. Gold is considered the best way to save the extra money that you have, and even it is "partially" better than real estate. That is due to its light weight. If you save your extra money in form of a property or apartment, you logically will not be able to take it to another country, while gold is very easy to carry and transport.

Gold is known as "safe haven" as people resort to it whenever a global crisis occurs. It is a rare mineral and with the rapid increase in the number of people around the world, the demand for gold increases and consequently the continuation of its price increases. It is also possible to divide the gold if you are selling it, you can just sell 100 grams or even less, but in condition of real estate, you cannot do that, you will just have to sell the whole apartment.

Despite that, we cannot say that gold does not get affected by declines or rises in the stock market, this may result in potential losses. The thing that prevent us to say that gold is the absolute investment option for you, but these losses can still be minimized to nearly zero when following advices of experts and accurate monitoring to the market. For example, during the current pandemic, all these fears represent a real opportunity for some gold investors.

And talking about currencies, especially the dollar, we cannot deny that it is the most powerful currency right now, but at the end of the day it is still a paper, and the strength of this particular paper is directly dependent on the strength of the United States, as the country moves politically and economically. Dollars are good if you intend to save, but given the current pandemic we may recommend gold first then real estate.

Chapter 7

Various ideas for "Online" Work – Invest in Yourself

Most people are still sitting at home because of the quarantines, to avoid gatherings and further spread of COVID-19. The imposition of the ban has caused many people to lose their jobs, and some have cut their salaries by nearly half.

The job market no longer depends on only the office system, but you can work from anywhere as long as you have a computer or a mobile phone connected to the Internet.

Teaching skills

If you master a manual skill, you can teach it to people by creating educational lessons for them and posting them on YouTube, or on your own blog, you can create them through the "Blogger" service provided by Google.

So if you master writing or even drawing on cloth, you can start creating lessons to teach those looking to master this profession, it is possible to allocate your lessons to a certain type of clothing, such as children's clothes, women, or evening clothes only.

- Drawing is also another skill if you are good at it, you can start teaching it online, and search for new ideas you can implement.

- Home solutions to daily problems in the kitchen, clothing, etc. If you are able to find easy and quick solutions, you can publish them on the Internet for the public to benefit from them.

-You can also start cooking lessons from inside your home, you do not need a professional camera to implement the video, but rather a mobile with a good camera and learn how to adjust the video.

- If you master a second language other than your original language, then you can start lessons to teach it through YouTube as well, there are thousands of people wanting to learn a second language.

Selling skills

Not only can you post and teach lessons, but you can sell your products to whoever wants them.

You can sell your meals and convert your kitchen to a small restaurant, or sell the clothes you create at home, as well as pictures that you design and display to specialized companies or individuals who want to advertise their products in a new way, or start selling your services in translation from one language to another.

Sales

If your skills are the ability to persuade and talk to people, you can register on the sites that specialize in selling products, you can offer the service of working with them as a seller.

Then you can promote their products and persuade customers to buy in exchange for a certain percentage determined by you.

- Accounting

If you are good at accounting, offer your services to some companies and start your work in the field of accounting from home. The field is no longer dependent on paper and pen, but rather specialized programs that can be run from anywhere.

- Decorations

If you are good at drawing, and you can work on interior or exterior drawing programs for installations, contact the specialized companies or use specialized sites in this field and offer your work to them for profit from everyone who buys the design from you.

- YouTube

YouTube is a big open for everyone, so you can record your own diaries, or make entertaining or educational videos, or even teach people something new (there are channels that specialize in education and teaching only).

Think carefully about something you master, and you can introduce it to the audience, and start a new and different job, to increase your income

Chapter 8

Experts' advices and overview

Usually history repeats itself whenever events are the same, which is well understood by big investors who are saving liquidity in times of crisis so that they can pick up stocks of collapsing companies, which have promising gains.

Promising opportunities

Coronavirus or COVID-19 which spread in the world and cost many companies 25-50% or more of its value, now offers promising opportunities for wealth creation, but it is also fraught with risks.

This was highlighted by billionaire Howard Marks, his company analysts and investment managers who work to register the shopping list in the collapsed stock market, but he advised his colleagues to use a defensive style and be patient when buying from collapsed markets.

According to Forbes magazine, Marks said in his speech to clients: "You may or may not feel there's still time to increase defensiveness ahead of potentially negative developments. But the most important thing is to be ready to respond and take advantage of declines."

The "Fear Index" on the American Stock Exchange is jumping at its highest pace in 5 months

Marks also explained at a meeting that the best prospects for investors are that the health system will succeed in containing the spread of the virus and treating patients, and then the economy will return to its previous condition.

In light of this, Marks expects stocks to continue falling, noting that we may not feel that there is a possibility to build a defensive plan in anticipation of any negative developments, but the most important thing is that you must be ready to respond and take advantage of the stock decline.

More severe than the global financial crisis

Marks recalled the memories of the global financial crisis in 2008 as he feared the crisis would spin out of control as we monitor containment measures in an economy that suffers from several bankruptcies within the field of financial companies, but life has not changed from what it was, and of course there was no danger to our lives.

However, he believes that the negative repercussions of the Coronavirus are more serious, as a result of social isolation, disease, death, economic downturns, almost complete dependence on governments, and lack of knowledge of the long-term impact on all of us, but the most important thing is to know when is the end of this crisis and what will be its consequences.

Containment and financial support first

Many of the big investors and analysts offered similar opinions. During their recent meetings on CNBC, two hedge fund legends: Paul Tudor Jones and David Tipper made clear that they needed containment and financial support in order to be able to get back into the market.

Tudor Jones was able to protect his company from the Coronavirus because he was monitoring its prevalence in China during January and February 2020, so it is likely that the same analytical perspective will be able to know when the recovery phase begins. Key to note that recovery phases will also vary across different countries, depending on how fast they contain the virus. Tipper closely monitored the impact of various government support methods on companies and financial markets.

In a research meeting, DoubleLine Capital CEO Jeffrey Gundlach shared an analysis indicating that markets may offset their losses last March.

All investors are still trying to deal with the effects of the pandemic. Will unemployment rise by 10% or 20%? Will GDP shrink by the same percentage? All of these questions have no answers and it will be different across many countries.

Conclusion

We must understand that the method used by some governments to raise awareness of the disease and the spread of it is sometimes exaggerated in order to use the method of shock with people, that is to ensure their quick adherence to the government's instructions on the necessity of adhering to home and health authorities' guidelines on preventing the spread of the disease.

And this is what we actually saw in the British Prime Minister's speech Boris Johnson when he said to the citizens to be prepared to lose loved ones and as we also saw in the speech of US President Donald Trump when he said prepare for hard days to come on the Americans, this is normal and justified but it should not be reflected in the smart investor's behaviour that puts things in its natural perspective and does not make investment decisions that may be affected by media.

Finally, dear reader, I do not underestimate the impact of this crisis on the economy but, we must be more aware and careful in choosing the source of information. Not to exaggerate the size of the impact. So that we do not see an unjustified panic in dealing with our investments, such as what we saw in consumer behaviour in the purchase and storage of food and spending huge sums on it despite its abundance. We should not underestimate the impact of government contributions to support the economy.

Here we listed our thoughts to grow your money through this hard time or at least to avoid the loss as much as possible, thanks for reading and best wishes!

Bibliography

Forbes. Billionaire Howard Marks Pitches A Defensive Investing Outlook. https://www.forbes.com/sites/antoinegara/2020/04/01/billionaire-howard-marks-pitches-a-defensive-investing-outlook/#31da27881324.

KENOSIS BOOKS: INVESTING IN PRECIOUS METALS SERIES

If you are looking for investment that offers you inflationary protection and that reduces your investment risk significantly, precious metals such as gold, silver, and platinum (amongst others) is the way to go. Unlike paper money, precious metals have a finite supply and you cannot print more of them, and because of this, precious metals offer authentic insurance against political and financial upheavals. This book will share about the ff:

WHAT ARE PRECIOUS METALS?
WHY YOU SHOULD INVEST? - THE UPSIDE AND DOWNSIDE
WHO SHOULD INVEST?
WHAT PRECIOUS METALS SHOULD YOU INVEST IN?
WAYS TO INVEST IN PRECIOUS METALS
CONCLUSION- WHEN SHOULD YOU INVEST?

The primary aim of this eBook is to open young investors' eyes to the infinite possibilities of investment in precious metals. This eBook shows you that you have the time advantage of youth and the ability to take on more risks, and that these advantages can help you make better and bigger investment profits, whether you choose to invest in gold, palladium, copper, silver, or platinum and whether you choose to invest in coins, bars, rounds, or precious metal ETFs.

So take action, and scan the QR CODE and/or Subscribe to our newsletter for more updates!

ABOUT THE AUTHOR

M. L. Pilgrim lost millions when he was starting as an entrepreneur but only his consistent belief in the power of the subconscious mind has brought him to his success. He is very active investing with majority of his portfolio in precious metals and stocks. Also, he invests in bonds, mutual funds, UITFs, and in other businesses in real estate, power generation, banking, logistics, retail, and telecommunications.

He worked across 10 countries always fascinated with the beauty of nature, culture, and traditions. He is a versatile author writing both fiction and non-fiction. He is a traveler, a dedicated father, a loving son, and a responsible brother.

He strongly believes that everyone can succeed both in business, relationships, society, and other aspects if they only have the right information and knowledge on how to use that information properly.

M. L. Pilgrim uses a pen name as he doesn't want to show himself as a definitive expert. Instead, he is in this journey with his readers like a "pilgrim" and wants to travel with them and share their experiences.

Reach M. L. Pilgrim in mlpilgrim.author@gmail.com. Cheers!

Or subscribe to his newsletter for latest updates on his investment books.

BOOKS BY THIS AUTHOR

THE PEOPLE'S GOLD: EVERYONE, EVERYWHERE, EVERY TIME! A Beginner's Practical Guide on All You Need to Know on How to Profit from Gold (Bonus! Practical Tips in Investing in Silver)

Don't have gold in your investment portfolio? Here's why you're missing out.

Is gold just for the rich?

Is it irrelevant in this highly digital economy?

Will it be of any use to your already diversified portfolio?

With prices at thousands of dollars for a few grams, gold is an expensive element.

You'd have good reason to believe that it's only something the wealthy would buy, and probably just as a part of their collection of expensive things.

But gold is much more than a material for luxurious jewelry or for ornate decorations.

Nowadays, gold is considered a safe haven for investors in an increasingly volatile market.

Some investors invest in gold when they foresee a recession, inflation, or uncertainty. Others hold on to gold to preserve wealth, while having a vehicle to pass it on to future generations.

In short, because uncertainty is inherent in any investment and in any economy, gold can serve as insurance in case of economic or political disasters.

Even in a highly digitized economy, gold continues to be attractive because it's a tangible asset that can still be of value, even if our entire monetary system collapses.

Fortunately, gone are the days when you had to pan for gold in a river, under the heat of the sun, with the possibility of ending up with nothing but a severe sunburn.

In today's economy, gold is easier to access and more affordable as well.

There are several ways to invest in gold that require nothing more than a computer, an internet connection, and a reasonable amount of money.

Don't lose out on the benefits of gold in your portfolio, even if you don't have billions of dollars to spare.

In *THE PEOPLE'S GOLD: EVERYONE, EVERYWHERE, EVERY TIME!, you will discover:*

- A **step-by-step guide** to getting started with gold investments, which you can follow even without any investing background
- How to legitimately invest in gold with **less than $100**
- **How much of your portfolio to invest in gold** so you don't lose out on market gains, but you still protect yourself enough in case of a severe downturn
- An **easy and accessible way to invest** in gold without having to worry about storage and theft
- How to tell real versus fake gold, and other smart ways to **protect yourself from gold scammers**
- Have a better understanding of your profile as a gold investor
- The varying reasons for investing in gold, and how they affect your investment strategy

- Know the different types of gold investors and see which one you can identify yourself the most
- **Bonus chapter**: Practical tips for investing in silver that could augment your portfolio even more

And much more....

Whether you think the economy as we know it will collapse in the foreseeable future, or you're just looking for a hedge against low interest rates, gold offers you this protection and more.

Even if you think your portfolio is already diversified enough, with stocks, bonds, real estate, and more, gold can still make a valuable addition to your portfolio.

Its unique qualities & ability to hedge against both equities & fixed income securities offer an extra layer of diversification & protection, especially for the most extreme cases.

Don't wait until the economic system collapses. Get some gold now and ensure that you're financially protected in case anything ever happens.

If you want to protect your finances & prepare for an uncertain future with a tangible, safe, & reliable asset, then click the "Add to Cart" button right now!

Best Ways to Invest Money During COVID-19: Make Money at Home

There are many things we can do during the pandemic and the most productive of all is to invest it wisely. Check out this book for some tips and guidance.

Best Ways to Invest in Gold For Beginners: Quick Guide for Learning and Investing in Gold. (BONUS: 14 Ways to Establish Real Gold from Fake Gold and more!)

Gold has kept a great value for thousands of years, and until this day it still occupies this high position, due to its properties that make it at the forefront of precious metals.

As it still retains its value throughout the ages, and the belief that is embedded in people's minds is that gold is the only way to pass and conserve wealth from one generation to another.

In times of political and economic tension as well as natural disasters, investors resort to buying gold as a safe haven in the markets and as a store of value, and it is also used as a hedge against high inflation. If you want gold to be part of your investment portfolio, you can choose from several investment options in gold, each of which has different investment characteristics. In this book, we offer many ways to invest in gold, tips to make the greatest possible start and the guide by which you can avoid fraud. We hope that we could help you, best of luck!

Best Ways To Invest In Silver For Beginners (Bonus: Nice Few Tips And Warnings On Investing In Silver

What do you know about investing in Silver?
The decision to start a project or take the first steps in the path of investment may be difficult but choosing the right investment and the field that matches your ambitions and needs is much more difficult. Perhaps this fear comes from the idea that you are here at risk of loss. You can easily lose everything that you have gathered in your life, but there is always light in the midst of all this.

Silver is not very much traded in the world, but because people love imitation . "See, this person has succeeded in trading gold, let's be gold traders like him." This is the main reason for loss. Success stories and money of others tempt you, so you start running towards it without awareness even though there are hundreds of fields to choose from.

In this book, we will show you the most important points, methods, strategies and tips that will give you the best start as a silver trader. Outlined among the chapters of this book, you will learn about silver investing across the following topics:

√ **Advantages** of Trading in Silver

√ **Disadvantages** of Trading in Silver

✓ Is trading in Silver **Profitable**?

✓ How to Start the Business?

✓ Where to Trade Silver?

✓ **Silver Trading Strategies**

We did not write these tips in a night or two and did not discover them by chance, we have already encountered them and have proven their effectiveness, and we have already seen many amazing stories thanks to them and we would like to give you the opportunity to be among them, use your chances in life!

So, grab a copy now of this book and check out our exciting bonuses and free books that you can avail!

Don't Forget to <u>Claim</u> your FREE ebook!

KENOSIS BOOKS: BE THE BEST YOU SELF-IMPROVEMENT SERIES

M. L. PILGRIM

S. K. PILGRIM

I.K. BUTCHER

KENOSIS BOOKS: BE THE BEST YOU – SELF-IMPROVEMENT SERIES

SUBSCRIBE AND GET YOUR FREE eBOOK!

If you want to improve the quality of your attention and are willing to do other means to improve your focus and concentration, then this book will definitely help you in that. This book contains the ff:

1. Top Foods to increase your Focus and Concentration

2. Foods you can intake daily to improve your focus

3. Best Juices to Improve your focus

4. Healthy Habits and Eating Style to Improve Focus

..... and much more!

So take action, and scan the QR CODE and/or <u>Subscribe</u> to our **Kenosis Books - Be The Best You: Self-Improvement Series** mailing list and be updated in our latest books and promotions!

How to Understand The Subconscious Mind: Unlock, Unleash, and Let it Transform You!

What do you know about the subconscious mind?

Do you want to know more about its characteristics? It is within us, but it is elusive in many aspects. So, careful understanding of the subconscious mind will bring us many benefits.

This book will share about the ff:

- What is the subconscious mind?
- Its relationship with the conscious mind
- Methods of connecting with the subconscious mind
- Secrets of the subconscious mind
- The rules of the subconscious mind
- Using your subconscious mind to achieve your goals
- Programming the subconscious mind
- How to achieve sleep miracles
- Controlling your subconscious mind

So, what are you waiting for? Check out this informative yet insightful book in unleashing this mysterious power within ourselves.

How to Thrive in Awkward Conversations: Learn the Art of Speaking with Skill and Consideration (BONUS! 10 TIPS TO IMPROVE YOUR CONVERSATION SKILLS!)

Have you ever found yourself in the middle of an Awkward Conversation?

Conversation is an art of dealing and communicating with others. Effective Communication aims to build understanding and acceptance - not conflict. However, there is that other type of conversation - *the awkward conversation.*

When you are in the midst of an embarrassing moment, you see yourself in a situation you wished you were not. Hence, knowing what to do exactly in those moments will prepare you for the worst.

This book will help you on the ff:
- Importance of Speaking Tactfully
- What makes conversations awkward and how to avoid them?
- How to have perfect conversation with your partner?
- How to handle a conversation with your parents?
- Business and work conversations
- General Tips and Tricks to be a top speaker

Grab a copy of this book and start your journey into more assertive, confident, and tactful!

How to Say No to Yourself: Conquering Intermittent Fasting 101- The #1 Complete Guide for Beginners & Busy People (Bonus: No-Stress 30-Day Simple Plan, Meal Preparations, Cookbook and more!)

Intermittent fasting is currently one of the most popular health and fitness trends in the world. It will teach you the unique process of following alternative fasting and feeding cycles.

This book contains proven steps and strategies on how to intermittently fast for weight loss and also examines the concept of clean nutrition.

By reading it, you will learn practical and proven arts and practices that, if followed religiously, will create a young, vibrant, exuberant, radiant and totally different being.

Do you have to lose weight? Are you trying to adapt to that new outfit for the summer? But you don't want to fall in love with those diets and lose weight with the quick tricks of the past, you need something that really stands the test of time. Much more than a diet, you need a change in lifestyle. This is exactly what the 30-day intermittent fasting challenge offers. Intermittent fasting can restart and restore the body, helping to put metabolic processes back on track. Fasting teaches your body to burn fat instead of complex carbohydrates.

With your body poised and ready to burn fat for fuel, stubborn fatty deposits like your belly, arms and legs will evaporate quickly! It may sound too good to be true, but only by regulating the body through a dedicated and consistent fasting regimen - this is truly possible! This book provides you with the knowledge, background, and recipes to successfully perform your intermittent fasting regime over the course of 30 days.

In this book you will get:
Why fast?
What is intermittent fasting?
Intermittent fasting and your hormones
Intermittent fasting and weight loss
Eat Healthily
The Keto diet
Autophagy and intermittent fasting
Pagan's diet
Intermittent fasting methods
Intermediate fasting benefits
Dangers of intermittent fasting
Intermittent fasting programs

And, in essence, everything you need to learn how to apply the practice of intermittent fasting to your life program to reap immense intrinsic benefits and thus become a healthier, happier, better and, yes, richer being.

The Adventures of Sephas (Simple Bedtime Stories for Kids: Quick Read and Illustrations Included): The Boy who Speaks 100 Languages and Helps Many People All over the World

It is his 7th birthday, he got a gift. Little did he know what this gift can do for him ... Where will he go? What can he do? Can Sephas save the day?

ABOUT THE AUTHOR

S.K. Pilgrim loves nature, travelling, food, and learning. He is a sport buff and loves running a lot. As a marathoner, he believes that keeping himself in good shape not only improves his running but also other aspects of his life. He loves reading books as well as writing them.

S.K. Pilgrim has a full-time job as senior leader in a multinational company. He is very passionate in coaching, training, and organizational development. He never gives up on any talent until they progress and improve to their potential!

Reach SK Pilgrim and our other authors in kenosisbooks@gmail.com
Cheers!

BOOKS BY THIS AUTHOR

<u>GIGA-ENERGY: High Energy Food - Turn-away from Sweets and Energy Drinks BONUS: Low Cholesterol and Low Sugar Energy Boosters</u>

LOW ON ENERGY? HOW LONG CAN YOU SUSTAIN YOUR ENERGY?

Daily tasks and labor require a lot of energy but ending up on the vicious cycle of coffee, sweets, and high-energy drinks is detrimental to our health.

This book aims to share with you alternative sources of energy that will make you more energetic and last longer through more sustainable and healthy means.

- Instant Energy Boosters
- Long-term Energy Boosters
- Plant-Based Energy Boosters
- Juices and Smoothies Energy Boosters
- Daily Routines to Maintain Energy Levels
- Faster Metabolism and Weight Loss
- Energy-packed Breakfast
- and Much Much More!
- BONUS

- Low-cholesterol Energy Boosters
- Low-sugar Energy Boosters

Grab a copy of this book and let it lead you to GIGA-ENERGY lifestyle!

ABOUT THE AUTHOR

I.K. Butcher's passion for building a conducive workplace started when he was in university. He began studying people development and practiced it firsthand. He led teams not only into developing themselves but also directing them into purpose – most especially, the socially oriented one.

Butcher continued this passion when he moved to a consumer goods company after he achieved his university degree. For 12 years, he learned sales, capability building, and business development. He travelled to various places both domestically and internationally to hone his skills and share his lessons to new employees who have begun in their careers.

Butcher believes that one needs to learn multitudes of skills to really excel in an organization and that he is very much willing to share his experiences to help those who are really serious about such an endeavor.

Reach I. K. Butcher and our other authors in kenosisbooks@gmail.com!

BOOKS BY THIS AUTHOR

MANAGING UPWARDS: THE BEGINNER'S GUIDE IN MANAGING YOUR BOSS (BONUS: THE SOFT SIDE: HOW TO WIN YOUR BOSS BY BUILDING A FRIENDLY RELATIONSHIP)

Have you been struggling with your boss? Are you a start out with the management skills to workplace excellence? Do you simply fancy the topic and wish to be armed with the artillery for Managing your Boss?

Whatever the category you find yourself in, this book is poised to arm you with all the necessary strategies for starting and maintaining a healthy and synergistic relationship with your boss in such a way that your personal goals, that of your boss, and the overall objectives of your company are met.

Outlined in well thought of moves, you will be led through four exciting journeys of

✓ Self-identification, skill discovery and skill optimization

✓ Identifying the personal traits, strengths, weaknesses, and context of your boss

✓   Knowing the company, what it stands for, your role and that of your boss

✓   Bridging the gap where stark differences exist

The major chapters all end with action points, step to take to ensure proper use of the information you're provided with. For the young, for the experienced, for whoever seeks to stand out and succeed in the workplace, this is the book for you.

So, grab a copy now of this book and check out our exciting bonuses and free books that you can avail!

Don't Forget to <u>Claim</u> your FREE eBook!

www.ingramcontent.com/pod-product-compliance
Lightning Source LLC
Chambersburg PA
CBHW071123240526
45465CB00023B/782